The Mantra Is a Prayer to God

Written by Ceci Miller

Illustrated by Laura Trayser

A Siddha Yoga® Publication
Published by SYDA Foundation

Published by SYDA Foundation
PO Box 600, 371 Brickman Rd, South Fallsburg, NY 12779-0600, USA
845-434-2000

www.siddhayoga.org

ACKNOWLEDGMENTS

With love and gratitude to all the people who offered their talents and expertise in creating this book:
Ceci Miller for writing the text; Laura Trayser for illustrating the cover and inside pages; Lori Fulsaas for cover and text design;
Cheryl Crawford for designing the hardcover edition; Julie Johnson for art direction; Paul Souza and Bruce Decker for design production;
and Karen Swezey, Patricia Stratton-Orloske, and Barbara Yaffe for overseeing production of the hardcover edition.
To everyone who helped with the editorial and review process—both the young and the young at heart—many, many thanks.

The poetry in this book was inspired by the grace-filled words of Gurumayi Chidvilasananda, which appeared in the book
We Have Met Before, about the 1996–1997 Siddha Yoga meditation world tour.

—Christine McNally, editor

Printed in the United States of America

First published in softcover, 1998. First hardcover printing 2000

06 05 04 03 02 01 00   6 5 4 3 2

ISBN 0-911307-92-3

This book is printed on recycled, acid-free paper.

About the Mantra

The mantra *Om Namah Shivaya* is a gift from the living master of the Siddha Yoga lineage, Swami Chidvilasananda, also known as Gurumayi. A mantra is a divine sound with the power to protect and bring joy to the one who repeats it.

The practice of mantra repetition is known as *japa*. Sometimes japa is done using a japa mala, a bracelet strung with special beads. The one doing japa repeats the mantra as each bead is touched. Through repetition of the mantra, we access its power and protection in our daily lives.

When reading this book with your child, you can repeat the mantra at the end of each page, and this will bring the practice of japa into the reading.

To all children everywhere

May your life always glow
with the golden rays of the mantra.

The Siddha Yoga meditation mantra is *Om Namah Shivaya*.

First *Om*, then five more sounds, *Na mah Shi va ya*.

Om Namah Shivaya. I honor God within myself.

The sound of the mantra is everywhere.

The mantra is a prayer to God.

Every breath is a prayer.

The mantra is like a big drink of delight.

The mantra tickles as it blows through the air.

The mantra makes me want to take flight!

The mantra helps me soar toward the light.

The mantra can bring peace and hope

And leave a trail of blessings to be found.

The mantra gives the nectar of love.

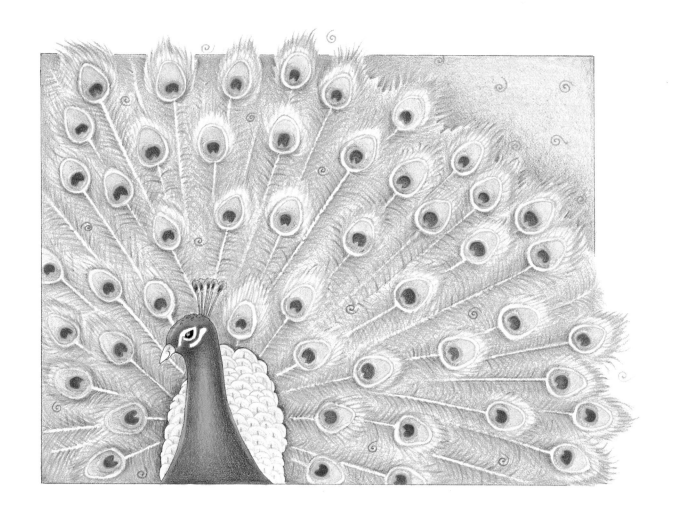

The mantra spreads beauty all around.

The mantra fills me with joy till I burst!

When the mantra pours out blessings, we sing.

The mantra is a waterfall. It washes over me.

The mantra is a jewel in the dark that gleams.

The mantra comes with me wherever I go.

The mantra gives courage, each time it is said.

The mantra is a safe and cozy home.

The mantra feels like a kiss on the head.

When I quietly listen in a soft still place,
I can hear the mantra humming through space.